The Invisible Laws of Money

The Invisible Laws of Money

Your Guide to Improving Everyday Financial Decisions

Richard Glenn Jones

Copyright © 2021 by Richard Glenn Jones

All rights reserved.

No portion of this book may be reproduced in any form without written permission from the author, except as permitted by relevant copyright law.

This publication is sold with the understanding that the author is not rendering legal, financial, investment, accounting or other professional advice.

The views and strategies contained herein may not be suitable for your situation. You should consult with a professional when appropriate. The author shall not be liable for any losses or damages whatsoever.

CONTENTS

Part I – Introduction 1
   Why I Wrote This Book 2
   What This Book Is About 4
   What This Book Is Not About 5
   This Book's Central Lesson 7

Part II - The Basic Principles Of Money 9
   Defining The Terms *Cost* And *Value* 10
   Understanding *Cost* Versus *Value* 12
   The Time Value Of Money 15
   The Relative Merits Of Opportunity Cost 18
   The Effects Of Price Inflation 19
   The Value Of Cashflow Certainty And Timing 22
   The Magic Of Compound Interest 26
   Small Sums Become Big Sums Over Long Periods 28

Part III - Practical Examples Of Hidden Cost And Value 30
   The Total Cost Of A Purchase 31
   Last Second Extras 38
   Free Money For Your Pension 43
   Proliferating Subscriptions 50
   Avoiding Complex Deals: The Case Of Car Finance 55

A Word About Vehicle Depreciation............57

Cash Purchase Of A Car 59

Hire Purchase 60

Leasing Or Personal Contract Hire (PCH)....62

Personal Contract Purchase (PCP).................65

Final Comments On Financing Options........67

Part IV – Key Takeaways................................69

Small Sums Become Big Sums 70

Cost And Value Are Different Things 71

What's Good For Business Isn't Necessarily Good For You 72

Conclusion 73

PART I – INTRODUCTION

WHY I WROTE THIS BOOK

Many years ago I earnestly (some would say naively) walked into a local firm of financial planners and asked what kind of help they might be able to offer me for my financial planning. The suited young gentleman asked me if I had a lump sum to invest. I said, no, isn't that what financial planners do? Help you plan your finances so you can build up a lump sum?

Needless to say, I left their offices a bit dismayed and embarrassed. I talked to my wife that night and asked rhetorically where ordinary people were supposed to get guidance and mentoring on their finances. They certainly don't teach this stuff at school. How do you get the benefit of other people's financial expertise if you don't already possess significant sums?

This came at a time when I'd begun to take an interest in personal finance and I found myself reading books covering all the usual topics such as savings accounts, mortgages, insurance, budgeting, debt reduction and financial investments. I learned a lot from my reading and certainly made some judicious changes in my finances and my mindset.

This desire to understand how money works was one of the reasons I decided to go on to become a Chartered Accountant (see more about my firm at www.principia-accounting.com). I wanted to be in the know.

I wrote this book because it has been a long road for me to learn the lessons it contains. I wanted to create tools for others, especially non-finance people, to improve the quality of their day to day financial decisions. I wanted to do this in a way that is jargon free and easy to understand with no need for prior financial expertise.

WHAT THIS BOOK IS ABOUT

This book is about decision making. It is about acquiring tools to evaluate your financial alternatives in a more meaningful way. The chapters that follow highlight basic concepts about how money and business work, and then show how to apply these concepts to financial decisions in everyday life.

The principles are universal and apply everywhere and to all currencies. They are like acquiring different lenses with which to see your own finances. Using these lenses will increase your confidence in financial decision making and keep more money in your own pocket. It will also help you steer your long term finances in the right direction.

WHAT THIS BOOK IS NOT ABOUT

There are many contributing factors to an individual's financial circumstances. Some of these factors we can influence or control and some we cannot. We cannot control that some people are born richer than others nor can we control broader economic ups and downs. Those are circumstances we just have to work with.

There are other areas though that we can influence or control by being proactive and determined, areas such as managing our spending, increasing our savings or building up creditworthiness. These controllable aspects are important, but this book is not about spending or saving per se. There are already many good books on these basics of personal finance.

Nor is this book about giving advice on what choice you should make when faced with any given individual financial decision. Many times there is no "right" answer, but rather a spectrum of choices from which you select appropriately according to your current circumstances. In a nutshell, it is the ability to meaningfully compare your alternatives.

Sometimes it helps to simply rule out the obvious worst choice. And indeed money may not be the only or even the most important consideration in any given financial decision.

THIS BOOK'S CENTRAL LESSON

The overarching lesson is this: the sum of all your small, everyday financial decisions makes a huge difference in the long run. If you can improve those decisions now, even moderately, there could be significant improvements in your long term financial outcomes. This principle applies no matter what your financial starting point.

For most people there's no single decision in life that financially makes or breaks them. What makes a much more significant difference are the habits followed day in and day out. The sum total of these daily decisions and their consistent application over many years makes a significant positive or negative contribution to your financial wellbeing.

In Part II of this book I will examine several basic interrelated concepts about money that all finance professionals know and use to guide their work. Although you cannot see or touch most of what is described in that section, you should nevertheless treat the concepts as real - like gravity or air. They are not theoretical ideas or academic discussions. They are the actual rules according to which money behaves.

Then in Part III I will use those concepts as a foundation to discuss other practical considerations about how money and business work. The discussion will include numerous examples of hidden costs and hidden value, pointing out areas where these can be found along with suggestions of ways to avoid the costs and capture the value.

Part IV contains the key takeaways and then some final thoughts for the future. So if you want to follow the path to better financial decision making, then read on!

PART II - THE BASIC PRINCIPLES OF MONEY

DEFINING THE TERMS *COST* AND *VALUE*

Merriam-Webster defines the term *cost* as the price or the amount paid or charged for something. Indeed cost and price are often used interchangeably in everyday life, and certainly no one doubts the importance of price as a primary consideration in most financial decisions.

However, there are often costs of a transaction that are beyond the headline price paid. Those costs can be cash costs that are not readily visible, or they can even represent an invisible loss of value which itself becomes a de facto cost.

The first definition given by Merriam-Webster for the word *value* is the monetary worth of something. Another definition given is a fair return or equivalent in goods, services, or money for something exchanged. The second definition focusing on fair return gets closer to the core of what I will try to describe below. It prompts questions like what is the total value I'm providing in a transaction versus what I'm receiving, and how do you measure that value?

I therefore think of cost as the price plus anything else that takes away value from me. My definition of costs includes the following: 1. The visible, cash headline price paid in a transaction. 2. The unseen or difficult to see costs of a transaction. 3. Loss of value or potential value outside the price that is now unrecoverable, or value that accrued to someone else unnecessarily. My definition of value is what you receive in a transaction after you've accounted for all the above costs.

UNDERSTANDING *COST* VERSUS *VALUE*

One way to compare financial alternatives is to compare cost versus value. It is sometimes difficult to see the forest for the trees when faced with immediate spending decisions because our tendency is to go for the lower number. Say you need a car battery and you have gone to the auto parts store. The shop attendant says he has a battery for your car for $50 that will last one year. The attendant says there is also a battery for $100 that will last three years. It is sometimes hard in the moment to decide to spend $100 today as opposed to $50 today. But the best course of action if you can afford it, even if it causes a little bit of short term pain, is to purchase the $100 battery because it is better value. That's because despite the price being double, the battery lasts three times as long (assuming it does in fact last 3 years). This broad idea applies in most areas of consumer purchasing.

It is similarly good to be on guard for things like retailer offers that purport to give you "better value". Is it really better value to buy the 2 for 1 deal on sandwich meat? Well that depends on whether you will eat two packets. It's probably not a deal if you have to throw away the second packet because you didn't get around to eating it.

Is it better value to buy 50 toilet rolls versus 5 if they are discounted? From the customer's perspective, I would question whether it is actually a significant discount. On the one hand, toilet rolls don't have an expiration date like sandwich meat so you have the leeway to buy in bulk and use them as you get around to it. If you have a very large family, it may be perfectly reasonable to buy 50 rolls at a time. On the other hand, you might be a single person and find you are saving 2 cents per roll and that you are not very much better off buying 50 toilet rolls at a time than you are buying 5 at a time.

From the retailer's perspective, selling 50 rolls instead of 5 is great news. The customer has spent far more cash than they might have otherwise and has spent it earlier. That is the retailer's idea of the perfect sale! So the lesson is this: buying in bulk *may* be a good deal, but don't just assume it is. It is more often a revenue generator for the seller. Get out the calculator on your phone while at the store to find out what kind of value you are getting for the extra expenditure by comparing the prices on a per roll basis.

In the end, is there anything wrong with a single person buying 50 toilet rolls at a time? Of course not, as long as they understand that the increased cost may not equal increased value.

THE TIME VALUE OF MONEY

An important concept to understand about money is that it has an aspect that is related to the passage of time – a concept aptly called the *time value of money*. Despite this aspect of money being largely invisible, it still represents real value that can be gained or lost. So you say to yourself, what has this tenner in my pocket got to do with the clock ticking? A surprising amount you'll find!

Let's assume your neighbor says he'll give you $100 today or $100 one year from today. Most people will instinctively know that the value of $100 in your hand now is worth more than the value of $100 one year from now. From a money standpoint, why is *now* better?

One reason is the time value of money. You could have kept that $100 in a savings account earning interest for a year. Instead, your neighbor received the benefit of using the $100 for a year. In other words, there is value gained by having use of the cash, just as there is value lost by not having use of it.

Money has a value outside of its immediate ability to pay for things and this aspect of its value happens as time progresses. It is why you receive interest from the bank on your cash deposit – because they are compensating you for use of *your* cash over that period. When you borrow from the bank and pay interest you are compensating the bank for use of *their* cash.

Despite time value being mainly invisible, it is important to accept this basic financial principle as real and true because it is one of the foundations of understanding money. In other words, no cash may actually leave your bank account, but if you get paid one year from now instead of today and take no other action, you've lost some real value all the same.

To come back to my original question then, what does that have to do with the $10 in your pocket? Well, the longer you keep it as cash in your pocket (or under the mattress or buried in the garden), the more time value it loses because it is not being put to good use bearing interest or being used in some other productive way. The time value of that $10 is being lost day by day.

THE RELATIVE MERITS OF OPPORTUNITY COST

The next related idea is called opportunity cost. It is the simple idea that when you use money for one purpose, you have also foregone all the other ways you could have used it. That means that by choosing to spend your money one way, you are effectively choosing *not* to spend it some other way.

Using the above example, you choose to keep the $10 in your pocket. One other option is to put the $10 in a savings account and earn some interest. The interest you did not earn is called the opportunity cost of keeping the cash in your pocket. There are always other options you could have chosen, and the consequences of those other options need to be considered to form an accurate view of the relative merits of each of your financial alternatives.

THE EFFECTS OF PRICE INFLATION

This might seem like stating the obvious, but one basic attribute of money is its relationship to how much you can buy with it at any given time. This works together with the time value of money. What you can buy with $100 changes over time due to inflation, usually in the direction of being able to buy less goods. That $100 will continue to buy less over time until you do something productive with it. And similar to the time value of money, most of this process happens out of sight.

A simplified illustration of inflation looks like this. Over the next year prices for goods in the economy rise 5%. So today the new trainers you want cost $100, and in one year they will cost $105 due to inflation. If you receive the $100 today in the example above from your neighbor, you can buy the trainers today for their current price of $100. Or if you receive the $100 today and put it in a savings account at 5%

interest, you could buy the trainers in a year for $105, still without having to add any extra cash. However if you wait a year to get paid, you will have to add $5 of your own cash to afford the trainers (unless of course you're charging your neighbor 5% interest!). That additional $5 represents the cost to you of waiting a year to receive the $100.

Inflation can also appear in more subtle ways. In recent years there has been a phenomenon that some call "shrinkflation", which has the same effects as traditional inflation. This is when a manufacturer quietly shrinks the product packaging size while keeping the price unchanged. A similar tactic is "value engineering" where a food manufacturer changes the proportion of the main ingredients of a product to reduce the cost of production. So a producer of chicken nuggets might reduce the proportion of chicken in its recipe to make a cost savings that goes unnoticed by the consumer.

These practices are of course price inflation via the back door. Some would even say the practices are deceptive because customers are not often explicitly alerted when this happens. Either way, these are inflationary losses that happen and that you should be aware of.

On the other hand, inflation works in your favor in some cases. Consider a mortgage on your home. The prices of goods in the economy usually increase year by year, as do the value of your home and salary. But the amount of the debt on your home does not inflate like prices. The debt amount is effectively frozen in time at the price level existing when you took out the loan. This means that over the years your mortgage starts to feel smaller because the outstanding amount becomes less relative to the value of your home and because the monthly repayment becomes less each year relative to your salary.

But in most cases inflation works against you and often in undetected ways. That's why it's important to recognize and understand inflation in order to counteract its long term effects where possible.

THE VALUE OF CASHFLOW CERTAINTY AND TIMING

Cashflow certainty and timing are two more factors that need to be considered. How certain cash is to come in or go out is always an important consideration and affects the value of a given sum of money. In the example above, you have accepted some cashflow uncertainty if you choose to get paid $100 one year from now rather than choosing to get paid today. What if your neighbor changes their mind, loses their job, moves away or dies? That's the risk you take by waiting one year. That kind of risk is also a largely invisible aspect of money though many people intuitively understand the concept.

When I was growing up the lottery had two ways to get paid if you won: you could take the millions in one lump sum or you could take it in equal payments over 20 years. Imagine your choice: $1 million per year over 20 years or $20 million today.

Taking the money today removes the enormous cashflow uncertainty that exists over a horizon of 20 years. That gives you the opportunity to put the money to productive use by investing it, allowing you to get the full benefit of the time value of the money over the 20 years instead of someone else receiving that value. That means you receive all the interest and investment gains over the 20 years rather than just a portion. That in turn helps counter the negative effects of inflation, which is considerable over long horizons because clearly the $1 million you receive in year 20 would have much less buying power than the $1 million you receive in year 1.

In financial terms (and obviously with good financial management), getting the money now is clearly better. Do yourself a favor if you ever have the luxury of winning the lottery: take all the money now, get a trustworthy financial advisor and ensure the sums are managed wisely.

Generally, you should prefer to receive cash earlier and pay cash later, *all other things being equal*. What I mean is that it's best to stick to this guideline as long as it doesn't cost you significantly extra to do so. If paying an insurance premium up front saves money and you have the funds available, then it may be better to pay earlier in that case.

However, say you have returned an item to a retail shop, or an airline has cancelled your holiday tickets. If they ask whether you would like a refund or a credit, you get the most advantage from a refund because you get back use of your cash. Taking a credit allows the shop or airline to keep hold of your cash. Therefore those businesses get the benefit of its time value and can put that cash to productive use in the meantime.

The strength of the preference is related to the circumstances and the amount in question. On the one hand, if you are owed a $25 credit by a retailer and it is a near certainty in your mind that you will use that credit within the next week - then ok, it's not a big deal if you take the credit instead of cash. That $25 is not a lot of money for most people, and you will be using the credit soon enough anyway.

On the other hand, the advantage of applying this principle is more apparent in the second instance. An airline says they can credit or refund you $2,000 for your cancelled family holiday tickets, and you think you will reschedule your holiday in 6 months.

In cases like this, it's best to take the refund. Taking a credit hands over to the airline the time value of your money and improves their cash flow while reducing yours. Taking the refund is also better because life will happen in the meantime creating uncertainty as discussed above. Minds change, rules change, circumstances change, airlines go out of business – who knows what could happen 6 months from now. If you have a choice, then get the refund and keep the cash in *your* bank account until you are ready to spend it again.

THE MAGIC OF COMPOUND INTEREST

And speaking of interest, there is a reason why Albert Einstein (allegedly!) said that the most powerful force in the universe is compound interest. Even if he didn't say it, compound interest is pretty amazing especially when viewed over long time periods.

Interest comes in two broad forms. The first is called simple interest and the second is called compound interest. Simple interest is what you earn on the original amount you invest in a savings account. Compound interest is the interest you earn on your interest. Let me explain.

Let's assume you put $1,000 into a savings account at a 5% annual interest rate with the interest calculated monthly. The bank calculates the interest they owe you each month based on the balance in the account at the end of that month.

At the beginning of Month 1 you deposit the $1,000 and at the end of the month the bank adds on the interest. That turns your $1,000 into about $1,004.17, the $4.17 representing the simple interest you earned on your principal in Month 1. If you leave that interest in your account, then in Month 2 the same calculation happens again using the ending monthly balance of $1,004.17. The interest in Month 2 will total $4.18, 1 cent more than in the previous month.

Your balance at the end of Month 2 would then be $1,008.35. That is made up of the original $1,000 plus $4.17 of simple interest in Month 1, $4.17 of simple interest in Month 2 and $0.01 of compound interest in Month 2. The latter is the interest on your interest.

Of course in Month 3 you continue to receive simple interest on the original principal of $1,000 and you also collect interest on all the previous interest received thus far. So the monthly interest received in Months 1 to 6 increases like this: $4.17, $4.18, $4.20, $4.22, $4.24, $4.25. Those monthly increases in interest are the magic of compound interest!

SMALL SUMS BECOME BIG SUMS OVER LONG PERIODS

I can understand how that 1 cent increase in interest in Month 2 probably doesn't sound very magical on the face of it. I know you aren't going to retire on a few pence of monthly compound interest. But just stay with me here.

Let's reconsider the $10 in your pocket from above. The effect of inflation and the time value of money on that $10 is not very significant in the short term. Losing that little bit of value over the course of a few weeks or months is not actually a big deal. But small differences become big differences over the long term. Losing the time value of money on larger sums over the course of a lifetime *is* a big deal. The bigger the sums and the longer the period, the more difference it makes.

To illustrate, investing a lump sum of $1,000 that's compounded monthly at 5% annual interest over 30 years turns into almost $4,500. If the initial sum were $100,000, the balance would grow to nearly $447,000 over 30 years. That's $347,000 of interest!

Taking a long-term view of personal finances is not a way of thinking that comes naturally to most of us, and we are not taught how to think like this at school. Instead of considering the total price of a mortgage over 30 years, we usually think more about whether we can afford the monthly payment. Instead of taking advantage of the powerful long-term saving potential of a pension, we spend the cash today.

I know it's necessary to make ends meet, but at the same time it's important to recognize that short term thinking has a cost. It's essential to start viewing things in longer timeframes if you are going to guide your financial life in the right direction.

PART III - PRACTICAL EXAMPLES OF HIDDEN COST AND VALUE

THE TOTAL COST OF A PURCHASE

We've all done it. You book that cheap ticket on a low cost airline and head to the online checkout to be met with a barrage of subsequent choices that inevitably make the ticket a lot more expensive. Choices about your carry on, your checked bag, priority boarding, reserved seating, travel insurance. Then on the checkout page you find a laundry list of handling fees, service charges, airport taxes and "airline imposed fees" (whatever that is – isn't that supposed to be the fare?).

We all know from experience that it is the total cost at the end of the booking process that matters, not the headline price you see on the seller's homepage. You may have had similar experiences with other purchases such as hotel stays or concert tickets.

But there are other instances where determining the total cost requires a little more awareness on our part. We often think of purchasing decisions only in terms of how much the monthly payments are. That is certainly one valid and necessary way to assess a purchase, but let's have a look at other ways that could also be helpful.

Think about the car insurance payment options you usually have. You can either pay one annual sum up front or you can pay in monthly instalments. It seems more convenient to pay in monthly instalments but if you do, you have just effectively taken out a short term loan and all loans come with a cost.

Let's say your insurance premium renewal gives you the options of either making a $500 annual payment up front or paying $44 per month. Most of us are going to gravitate towards the $44 per month – it's a smaller amount and seemingly easier to cope with versus handing over $500 right now.

However if we look at the total cost of each option, we find that the first payment plan is obviously $500 in total annual cost. The second option is actually $528 in total ($44 x 12 months). That means it's $28 cheaper to make the annual payment. The second option then is a short term loan at roughly 5.6% annual interest.

And to continue with the notion that small sums become big sums over long periods, let's assess the total impact of the decision to continue taking out these short term loans every year. Imagine paying $28 extra every year for 30 years – that's $840. But if you were to put that $28 in a savings account at the beginning of each year at 5% interest instead of paying it to the insurance company, it would become nearly $2,000 over 30 years. Now imagine you did that every year with your house insurance and any other insurances.

I understand that not everyone is in a position to pay their car insurance annually. But you can see that it would be well worth doing so if you could plan your spending and saving in a way that would allow annual payments. You are not just trying to save a few random pounds here and there. You are literally transforming the way you conduct those transactions, choosing the option that works for you instead of the convenient option that works for the insurance company.

Looking at a similar example, let's say you are buying a mobile phone and you've narrowed the options to two tariffs. Both tariffs have the same phone and the same amount of data, calls and texts included. The first tariff is $50 per month for 24 months. The second tariff is $40 per month for 24 months but requires a $150 payment up front. Which one is cheaper?

The total cost for the first tariff is $1,200 ($50 x 24 months). The total cost of the second tariff is $960 ($40 x 24 months) plus the $150 upfront payment for a total of $1,110. So the second tariff is $90 cheaper over the course of 24 months. This is true despite having to pay $150 up front.

Of course, a small amount of time value is lost by handing over the $150 now compared to putting it in a savings account for 24 months (at 5% that would be about $15 of interest foregone). But even taking that into account, you are still saving $75. It is clearly cheaper if you can afford it to pay the $150 up front. Again, you are not going to retire comfortably on a one time savings of $75 but the cumulative effect of making decisions in this way over a lifetime is considerable.

Mortgages are also a case of where total cost is the only way to reliably compare deals. There is no reason to be anxious about doing the sums. There are lots of mortgage calculators on the internet (such as https://www.moneysavingexpert.com/mortgages/mortgage-rate-calculator/).

The key is that you look at the total cost over the entire term of the mortgage and consider that along with what you can afford each month. A mortgage calculator will take your proposed mortgage amount and interest rate and show you your monthly payment and the amount of the total interest you will pay over the course of the mortgage. The calculator lets you input the upfront fees for the mortgage as well. These need to be included in your calculation to calculate an accurate total mortgage cost, so never compare using only the headline mortgage rates.

Foreign currency exchange is likewise an area where comparison of the total costs of the transaction is the only accurate method of comparison. Exchange firms often advertise based on their exchange rates which is obviously an important number affecting how much you will have to pay. But there are often extra costs on top of the headline exchange rate that need to be accounted for. Any extra fees need to be taken together with the exchange rate before you are making valid comparisons.

The way to ensure you get the best deal is like this. If you want to buy $100 USD, then like with any purchase, you are looking for the lowest possible total price including all fees to obtain that currency. So if one firm charges £75 GBP for the $100 and another firm charges £80 GBP, then the £75 is the clear winner.

If you think of this the other way and you say to yourself, I have £100 GBP I'd like to exchange for US dollars, then the same principle applies in mirror image. In this case you want to know who gives you the most dollars after all fees. Then if you find that one firm provides

$130 for your £100 and the other provides $135, you'll know the latter is the better deal.

It's easy to get turned around when buying currency, so the key lesson is to always use total cost when comparing the alternatives and do your homework beforehand so you know what to expect. And I would add as a bonus that you shouldn't impulse buy foreign exchange at the airport. It's best to buy currency online beforehand to get the best rates!

LAST SECOND EXTRAS

A related issue to total cost is adding what I like to call last second extras. This is the practice of some companies of introducing last second decisions about the purchase to push up the total cost. Most of these decisions introduced at the last second are frequently high in profit for the seller and low in value for the customer. These items can significantly inflate the total cost of a good or service while adding very little value for the consumer. It pays to know what you want beforehand and to have the discipline to stick to your decision, therefore not falling prey to the tragedy of suggestibility.

I am not saying there is never an instance where some extra value can't be had by keeping your eye on the ball and making the occasional, judicious last second decision. I'm just saying there are some common last second decisions introduced into many consumer retail transactions where it would be wise to exercise caution.

This technique often happens when you buy an airline ticket online as discussed above. After you have spent significant periods of time planning your trip, searching for tickets, paying extra for your bags, and deciding whether it is worth paying extra for seats, you may then be presented with a decision like whether you want to buy travel insurance. The travel insurance offered at the last second while buying an airline ticket almost always comes at a high price with low value. If you want travel insurance, go to a comparison site online and see what is available in the market. You can often find much better coverage for less money that way.

This notion covers a lot of other areas as well. It could be upsizing in fast food restaurants to a larger meal at the last second when all you came for was a sandwich. Would you like a super-hot-flamin' order of Ranch chicken flippy dippers with that? As a general rule, the decision to say yes is bad for your health and the only thing genuinely super about the transaction is the increase in the restaurant's revenue and profit margin. All it really adds for you is extra cost and extra calories.

Avoiding last second extras also applies when you are offered insurance for electronics from the cashier when you're paying. This is often a bad idea. Look around on a comparison site online if you want insurance for your gadgets. You can probably get better insurance for less money elsewhere, and in some cases your home insurance may already cover household items such as this. I get the potential need for electronics insurance, particularly if you've got children, so I'm just suggesting doing your homework before committing to the last second coverage. You can always add it on later if necessary.

Additionally, online retailers often try to inflate the total cost by suggesting that "all these items frequently bought together" when you are on your way to the checkout and were only intending to buy one item. It's worth double checking if you really need those items before adding them to your shopping cart.

It could be opting for monthly charges when opening a new bank account that includes extra benefits and services. If these services will actually be of use to you, then that's fine. A benefit might be that you get a better interest rate on your balances (but you need to do the math to see if it is worth the extra that you are paying!). However, many times there are services attached to the account such as travel insurance or legal services that the customer will never use or that are not value for money, with a better quality service easily available elsewhere for lower prices.

Recently, there has been a new last second decision added to many transactions called Buy Now Pay Later (BNPL). This type of credit ballooned during the covid pandemic into a multi billion-pound market across a vast array of consumer products and services. Ostensibly it is credit with no interest and no credit check. What could be easier? Well probably nothing, but it could cost you dearly. Be sure you are not buying more than you can afford because the late fees for this type of "interest free" credit are eye watering. It could be better in the long term to use your own credit card or save up until you can afford it.

There are similar schemes with some online purchases where you are offered a significant percentage off the price of your purchase for applying for a credit card. If you need a credit card you should talk to your own bank first because it is rarely a good idea to opt for these unsolicited approaches for credit.

To sum up, if a shop or website is asking you to make a last second, on-the-spot buying decision, buyer beware. In that case, it is more often best to give it a miss because last minute extras often just cost extra while adding little value for the consumer.

FREE MONEY FOR YOUR PENSION

I'm well aware that when someone mentions "pension" in a conversation, it usually causes everyone in the room to head for the exit. It's the sort of thing that's a necessary evil at best. So bear with me while I explain what a pension does and then I'll get to the part about the free money.

A personal pension is a way to save money that allows you to pay tax later. That is the single outstanding advantage of most types of pensions: you don't pay tax now on the money you put in the pension and then you don't pay tax on any growth of the assets within that pension. In other words, you only pay tax decades later after you retire and start receiving income from those funds. That's quite a good deal.

I'm referring here to a personal pension, known as a defined contribution pension. This pension is the type in which the responsibility for overseeing the pension funds is yours. Contrast that with defined benefit pensions, also known as final salary plans. This is a plan where employers (which are often government organizations) are responsible for the ongoing performance and management of the pension fund. I describe the UK system below but the US system operates in a very similar way.

The way the cash usually arrives in a personal pension is that you and your employer both contribute money to it. I say "usually" because it is possible to put money into a pension without an employer although that's not the most common scenario. In the UK, you are automatically enrolled in your pension program when you are eligible and then re-enrolled every 3 years. Employers currently have an obligation to pay in a minimum of 8% of your basic salary into a personal pension, with the employer providing at least 3% and the employee providing the other 5%.

There is the possibility of "opting out" of pension contributions after you have been enrolled. To reiterate an earlier point, the following is not advice about your personal situation. Only you can make decisions about and take responsibility for your long term financial well-being. However, it's important to understand the consequences of opting out.

Should you opt out instead of making pension contributions, you will lose the free 3% your employer would have contributed. You also forfeit the long term, tax free growth of the entire 8%. That's called declining free money.

I know that there may now be a chorus of objections. Yes, you feel strapped. You have bills to pay. People will say they feel like they can't afford it, that they have mortgages to pay and children to feed. Those are all understandable responses because you do have to wait quite a long time to get the eventual benefit (at least until you are 55 in the UK when you can withdraw funds from a personal pension). All of that is true and I understand it because I certainly didn't grow up with a silver spoon in my mouth. I come from a solidly working class family.

But despite any protestations, opting out is still refusing free money. In the long term you are losing out on quite a lot actually.

I'll give you an illustration to demonstrate the principle. Say you earn a $25k annual salary and you put 5% of your pay into your pension each month (that is $104.17 per month before tax). Let's also assume that your pension grows at an average rate of 5% compounded monthly (which would be a historically low long term growth rate for most invested pensions). That formula would result in a pension balance of about $87k in 30 years' time.

Oh, but hang on! That's just *your* contribution, so let us add in the free money! Let's say the full 8% of your salary goes into the pension each month for 30 years (the 5% that you put in plus the 3% your employer puts in which totals to $166.67 per month). Let's assume the same growth rate of 5% as before. Your ending pension balance increases from $87k to nearly $140k. Obviously the figures will vary according to the growth rates assumed and the time periods covered. But in this example, you can easily see the large sums foregone by opting out of personal pension contributions.

Or you can still opt out. By doing that you do get the 5% cash each payday that you would have contributed to the pension, but the flip side is that you also have no funds working for you going forward. And you would have to pay tax on that cash *now*. If you are a basic rate taxpayer you would have to pay 20% in tax on that $104.17 per month plus 13.8% National Insurance to boot. This means, among other things, that the government gets use of that cash for the next 30 years instead of you. And you are left with barely $70 additional cash in each monthly pay packet.

The question is this: can you afford in the long term to miss out on the free money? Again, there may be some constraints in your circumstances, and it may take some rearrangement of your finances and your spending habits – and there are lots of good books out there written on these topics. But it is undoubtedly in the interest of the vast majority of people to take advantage of the free money and the tax advantages that come with a pension.

Where does the money go if you opt out? The employer literally keeps the money. Most employers want the best for their employees and would not actively encourage anyone to opt out. But when you do opt out, that represents a reduction in the payroll expense of the employer and increases their profit. And crucially, the cash they would have spent stays in *their* bank account instead of being transferred to *your* pension fund.

Making the leap on pension saving can be difficult because it comes with a double curse. It is hard to see the value you are losing when you are not contributing because that value is invisible. Similarly, it's hard to see the value you are gaining by contributing to the pension because it is also largely invisible. That's because the significant gains in this process only happen over very long periods of time and because the contributions grow in the background, out of sight of daily life.

So if you decide to contribute to your pension, it might be motivating to get the pension app and set a reminder on your mobile phone to check the balance every year so you can periodically enjoy seeing the free money working for you!

PROLIFERATING SUBSCRIPTIONS

Uncertainty is the enemy of business. Businesses prefer steady and predictable.

One way businesses like to increase certainty in their revenues and cash collection is by getting customers to sign up to subscriptions or some other type of recurring charges. That is why most subscriptions involve the seller taking your credit card details and you agreeing to them automatically taking a charge each month. Businesses call this monthly recurring revenue. This model makes it easier to keep customers because it is a system where the default position is customer retention. Contrast that to the traditional system where the customer has to actively choose to pay each month. This is an approach where the default position is customer loss.

Having customers on monthly subscriptions increases revenue, increases cashflow certainty, and allows for more accurate forecasts. That is very good for business but does create ongoing costs for you that just run in the background.

Take cloud storage for the data on your phone as an instance of this. When you sign up for recurring monthly payments for cloud storage for your phone, you are effectively agreeing to pay those recurring charges for at least an extended period if not for the rest of your life. That is because your storage needs are only going to get bigger. Spending 99 cents per month for cloud storage doesn't sound like a lot of money. However when you get tens or even hundreds of millions of people signing up for what could be the rest of their lives, all paying 99 cents per month - that turns into an extremely large revenue stream. I am by no means saying that you shouldn't get 99 cents a month cloud storage. I'm only pointing out the provider's viewpoint - that 99 cents per customer each month across millions of customers is a lucrative and steady business model.

Coming back to mobile phone contracts, when you sign up the provider will know that over the term of the contract your monthly subscription will come in at regular intervals. If you are on pay as you go, the supplier may have an idea what you might spend, but this amount is definitely going to be less certain than someone who is on a contract. That's because pay as you go gives you more control over the timing and amount of the expense. With a contract you have already agreed in advance the amount and the timing with the mobile company, and they very much prefer that predictability.

Ah, but you may say how do they know my direct debit won't bounce? Well, they don't know if your specific direct debit will bounce. But what they *do know* is that in their business an average percentage of direct debits bounce each month, let's say 1%. So in this way they are able to make rather accurate forecasts of their future monthly income based on assumptions like these.

The subscription model applies to many things: cloud storage, mobile phone contracts, phone app subscriptions, online retailer perks, video streaming, music streaming, e-books, audio books, e-learning websites, computer software. Businesses are continuing to expand subscriptions to everything under the sun: meal kits, gym facilities, access to cars, video games, education, well-being services, home maintenance, everyday household items.

To be clear, I'm not saying that subscriptions are always a bad idea. In many cases a subscription model can work for you too. With my own phone, I just want to be able to use it a reasonable amount each month without the hassle of recharging it and having to worry about whether I will run out of call minutes or data at an inconvenient time. I also don't want to have to pay my television streaming service manually every month. I know I am going to carry on watching it for some time to come. So subscriptions work for me in those instances.

But what I am saying is that subscriptions are super for business, and it is in your interest to keep that in mind as you make decisions. Have "no subscription" as your default until you can justify the cost versus value in your own mind. Make sure any subscriptions you already have represent value for you and that you review them regularly because once engaged they tick along in the background largely out of sight. Make sure you have subscription notifications turned on so that you are reminded each time a subscription payment is made. And never delay cancelling a subscription that you are not using anymore - even if it is only 99 cents per month. You already know that over time small sums become big sums!

AVOIDING COMPLEX DEALS: THE CASE OF CAR FINANCE

Warren Buffett, the legendary American investor, famously said he doesn't buy businesses he doesn't understand. The same advice should extend to many types of consumer purchases and especially to financial products. Financial products can range from straightforward to surprisingly complex. In my experience the more "convenient" they are, the more value you may potentially lose in the process. If there are lots of moving parts in the terms and conditions, then it might be better foregone for something simpler.

Let's have a look at a transaction most of us do numerous times in our adult lives: finance a car. Similar to car insurance financing where you pay interest for a "convenience", so it is with financing the car itself. There are several basic ways to finance a car as discussed below, and they are in order of progressive complexity with the simplest first. And as always, don't forget to use total cost to compare the different financing deals (within financing methods as well as between methods).

A WORD ABOUT VEHICLE DEPRECIATION

Depreciation in the value of a car (or any other asset for that matter) constitutes an invisible but real cost that needs to be taken into account. Depreciation is the amount an asset reduces in value as its useful life is consumed. This concept is often referred to as "wear and tear".

A car's useful life is usually measured in miles, and so the depreciation increases as you drive more miles and the value of the car correspondingly decreases. All other things being equal, the value of a car with 20,000 miles is clearly higher than a car with 100,000 miles. This principle applies to many other assets as well. An industrial machine's life may be measured in machine hours or a building's life may be measured in years. As the machine hours or the years accumulate and the useful lives are consumed, the depreciation steadily increases while the asset value decreases.

And an asset may not depreciate at a uniform rate across its life. A new car usually depreciates faster than an older car. Of course there's nothing wrong with buying a new car, as long as you understand that you lose more value through depreciation than you would on a used car. This is a point that should be considered alongside the discussions below in understanding the total cost of a car deal.

CASH PURCHASE OF A CAR

Obviously, the first and simplest kind of car financing is to buy a car outright with cash you have on hand. This method reduces financing costs by using your own cash instead of using someone else's cash. Using your own cash also results in more peace of mind due to owning a car that you can easily afford and on which you don't have to make ongoing payments.

One "negative" is that this method is not going to result in you driving a brand new flash car with all the bells and whistles. You will likely have an ordinary car that is a few years old. Another disadvantage is that you have to shell out cash up front for the entire amount of the car, although to be fair it's an amount you've already decided you can afford and you do receive a car that you will own outright in return for your money.

HIRE PURCHASE

Financing a new or used car can also be done via a process called Hire Purchase (HP). It is a little bit more complicated than buying for cash but is still a reasonable option for many people. It effectively allows you to spread the cost of owning your car over a period of time. You usually make a down payment up front (say, 10%) and then you make payments to pay off the rest of the purchase price over the next 2-5 years.

One advantage of this method is that you own the car outright at the end of the HP agreement. Additionally, HP financing can allow you to get a nicer car than you would be able to afford if you needed the entire lump sum of cash up front. The negatives are that there is an upfront deposit and a commitment to a multiyear financing contract. Additionally, although you don't technically own the car until the last payment is made, the maintenance and repairs are your responsibility while you are paying it off just as if you did own the vehicle.

If you are comfortable with the monthly payment and ongoing maintenance costs, HP can be a good solution for many people and often comes with reasonable interest rates on the money you borrow. But as always, compare the total cost of several HP deals (including administration fees) to get the bargain that is best for you.

LEASING OR PERSONAL CONTRACT HIRE (PCH)

The next financing option isn't particularly complicated, but the difficulty is that there could be more invisible value lost in this method. As discussed above, convenience costs money. This method is called leasing or is sometimes called Personal Contract Hire (PCH). It is important to note that this is not buying a car: it is effectively a long term car rental and you will not own it at the end of the contract.

The way this works is that you will likely pay the dealer or manufacturer lower monthly payments than you would if you wanted to own the car on HP. You get to drive a very nice if not new car and you could even pay a bit more per month to include repairs and maintenance in your monthly payment. At the end of the contract, the lessors get the car back and you may or may not be finished paying. There are often extra charges if you exceed the agreed maximum mileage and if there is any "damage or excessive wear and tear". You will also likely face charges if you want to leave the lease agreement early. After the lease is finished, what you effectively have left are happy memories of having driven a nice car for a few years.

The key advantage of this method of finance is that you get to drive a very nice car that you may not be able to afford otherwise. The main downside to this method is that there is no possibility to own the car at the end of the contract. It is only a long term car rental after all. You hand back the car and you are left with no value going forward for the money you have paid out during the lease. This is contrasted with HP where you own the car at the end of the financing agreement. Many explanations of leasing will pitch the fact that you "just hand back the car" at the end as one of the key benefits of this method when it could rather be construed as a drawback.

Driving a new car without the responsibility of owning it comes at a significant premium and will be more expensive in the long term than buying a car with your own cash or even via HP. This is likely true even if the monthly payments in the short term are lower. That's because this is best seen as an issue of cost versus value. Of course, the HP monthly payments will be higher than with PCH, but because you own the car at the end it will likely represent better long term value especially if you plan to keep the car for a few years.

It is true that there is a place for leasing vehicles, especially for businesses with large fleets or maybe some individuals who do a lot of driving for work purposes or entertain a lot of clients. But for many people, leasing a new car may be more of a lifestyle choice than a value choice.

PERSONAL CONTRACT PURCHASE (PCP)

The third financing method is called a personal contract purchase (PCP), and it is more complicated still with several moving parts. There are three main parts to a PCP contract: an upfront down payment (often 10% of the car value, similar to HP), the amount of money you are borrowing, and the final balloon payment at the end if you want to own the car. There is a calculation involving the estimated future value of the car and this determines the amount of the final balloon payment. Therefore the total price less the down payment, less the estimated future vehicle value, leaves the amount you will need to borrow and make monthly payments on.

A lease or PCH agreement only has one contractual outcome, and that is you return the vehicle to the lessor. On the other hand, at the end of a PCP contract you have 3 choices: you can just hand the car back similar to PCH, you can make the balloon payment allowing you to own the car, or you can roll over into another PCP contract and get a new car.

The interesting issue with PCP contracts is that most of them end with the car being handed back. I would argue that if you hand the car back on a PCP contract, then it has effectively been a lease/PCH agreement by another name. Usually PCP monthly payments are higher than PCH, so that means you are paying extra for options in a contract that you are unlikely to use. It's important to have a clear idea of your intentions at the start so you can avoid paying over the odds.

FINAL COMMENTS ON FINANCING OPTIONS

The financing options above represent methods that progressively increase in cost and complexity and often with the potential for loss of value. Cash is the easiest, simplest way of financing a car. HP financing is somewhat more expensive but has the advantage of getting a nicer car that you will own at the end for a reasonable amount of interest on a loan. PCH is very convenient and you will drive a very nice car, but PCH can sometimes represent a loss of invisible value compared to HP because you don't own the car at the end. PCP is more complex still and has a premium built into the cost of financing due to the options available – options that many people never use.

So if you are an individual who just needs a reliable car for the usual commuting, shopping and holidays, then think carefully before you enter into the more complex car financing options. But there is also a general underlying principle in this: The more complex an offer is, especially with regard to financial products, the more potential there is for losing value compared to simpler products that are easier to understand.

PART IV – KEY TAKEAWAYS

SMALL SUMS BECOME BIG SUMS

If you go away with a single idea at the end of this book, I hope it's the knowledge that small sums become big sums over long periods of time. Similarly, sustained small improvements in your decision making processes also become big improvements over long periods.

A long view is necessary to understand the huge benefits to be had by, for example, investing in a personal pension. The time element of money and wealth cannot be underestimated in this regard. Alongside this is other everyday habits such as ensuring that your subscriptions are working for you and avoiding excessively complex financing or investment deals.

COST AND VALUE ARE DIFFERENT THINGS

Remember that *cost* and *value* are different things and should not be conflated. Your cost may actually be more than the price you pay depending on the certainty and timing of the cash outlay, loss of any time value of money, opportunity costs, and effects of inflation. And just because there's more cost doesn't mean you're automatically getting more value.

It's almost always the total cost of a purchase that you need to review when making comparisons between financial alternatives and this includes ensuring you aren't taken in by last minute extras in your purchases unless they represent real value for you.

WHAT'S GOOD FOR BUSINESS ISN'T NECESSARILY GOOD FOR YOU

Finally, what's good for business and what's good for you are often two different things because businesses design models that benefit themselves. This is not meant to be a criticism, it's just how the world works. It's important to recognize when it doesn't work for you and to take action in your own interest if that's necessary.

CONCLUSION

Putting all this together, one useful way of making financial judgments is to use each of these lessons individually keeping all other variables equal. Doing this gives you several ways to look at a decision and can hopefully produce a more rounded perspective. It is a good way of judging the relative pluses and minuses of several alternatives. For instance, do I want to pay now or pay later? All other things being equal and assuming it does not cost me to do so, I would pay later.

But obviously these principles all work together in unison in real life and so there's no single formula for making all financial decisions. There are just broad strategies that you apply to understand each new decision as it arises, although you may over the years encounter similar situations and start to become familiar with what is best for you in those circumstances.

I hope that this book has introduced you to some better ways of viewing your financial life and wish you good luck. Acting on these ideas could be the next big step in your financial journey!

www.ingramcontent.com/pod-product-compliance
Lightning Source LLC
Chambersburg PA
CBHW070356230526
45471CB00006B/2591